Baptism by Fire

by
Amy-Jean Muller

Introduction by
Stoya

Close To The Bone Publishing

Acknowledgments

Thank you to the following people for your contribution to Baptism By Fire

To my family, thank you for your patience, encouragement and insight

A special thank you to Stoya, Pornographer and author of Philosophy, Pussycats, & Porn

To everyone who read, published and provided feedback on the work, including Ariana Den Bleyker, C. Cimmone, Travis Cravey, Fizza Abbas, Stephen J Golds, Craig Douglas and Holly Hunt (BA, MSt Greek and Latin Literature, University of Oxford)

To my editors, Craig Douglas and Stephen J Golds

To my publisher, Close to the Bone

To my readers

To every woman

For L.S.G.W

Brush me up like driftwood

for I am away with you my love

Index

Introduction by Stoya

Womanhood has long been associated with emotion. Sensitivity is correlated to femininity, which is correlated to weakness. But where's our anger? Patriarchy, a running theme—in this collection of poems and our lives—tolerates very little of it from the fairer sex.

But maybe "fair" here means judicious—righteously roused in response to unevenly distributed privilege and power. Justifiably resentful in the present tense.

Anger is active, assertive, and aggressive.

It demands. It provokes. It requires.

An angry woman remains a political act, and is sometimes a creative one as well. Rage, here, is transcended into art. It becomes constructive—clearing the way for growth. Fury is wielded as a transformative force. It burns away impediments to change. What blooms after?

1

Before I Was Born

She knitted me a blanket
between her finger and thumb
with thick protective strands
draped on her swollen belly
where I grew
And when Dad spoke,
tensions thread snapped suddenly
around the image of a
house illustrated in
appliqué stitch
Her fingers bled
on the broken needle
piecing the burgundy yarn
at hearing his words.
My blanket came undone the day
blood soiled the throw she made me
The utterance of my father said
I didn't ask you for this baby

Wooden Boxes

        Keep your hopes
small
        to fit the size of a shoe box
neat enough to hide below your bed
but big enough
to be crushed
by the heel of
        a Man's boot

Choked at birth

My birth was like a hanging;
breathless and suspended from her tree
I was thrust from her branches
with the cord wrapped twice
around my neck

My gasps sounded the moment,
Death and Life shook hands,
where cutting the cord
spilled a blood red ribbon
over their covenant

My future carved itself in wood,
burdened heavy like lumber,
marking the last time I would be stifled
Left roaring in the arms of
my weeping Mother

All the Little Children

Lamb of God
with fresh rosemary and wine
tastes just as bitter
            as the lies we tell little girls
serving Sunday dinner
after church
with prayers
            ending in a smile and
            A MEN

Sacrifice

We shared our lunches together on the Sabbath
eating ice-creams in the sheen of the sun.
Sweetness stuck to our fingers
running down to our elbows,
pressed with orange flavored kisses from our hands to our lips.
And when she told me to wait,
returning to the home of our Summer keeper;
She went towards him like a sacrifice
into the heat of his house
That summer was warmer than we felt in years
although the years weren't many between us Sister,
and we shared it together,
in the heat of that morning
with a heave in his house,
with those hands on our thighs.
Leaving orange flavored sticky
circling his pride

Father Forgive Me

    Jesus bled there
in front of me
strung up in the church where all their sins were freed
but mine
    And I was terrified that he'd come at night
under my bed
as a man,
to save me from something sinister
    he'd do himself

No More

                A swing rests with a rope frayed on the
edge of the garden
from the bare broken birch bough
reaching crooked up to heaven
sitting solitary
                there.
Without verdures
without laughter
the bench moves a whisper
in the sullen wind.
                Having once heaved my turbulence from its seat
as a girl child
                innocent
                and green.
But
in his pushing
a view up my skirt in the unrelenting gale
left sight
to navigate a pathway
for the hands of
that man,
to steer my laughter
                no more

What Are You Made Of?

Boys are made of slugs and snails
while girls are told outlandish tales
where sweetness rests in silent listening
and obedience wets the holy christening
of men who stand beside
the holy spirit
with God our father
and the priest we visit
but remember the trinity
and be silent girl too
they live up in heaven
where Men
also have rule

Roses

I met a father once
and he was different from mine
when he laughed at my jokes
looking at the buds that grew on my chest
pushing swollen behind the flesh
of a pink nipple
And when he handled them like roses
His fingers grasped my blossoms
to hear my wince
having taken a bouquet
of petals
from flowers
that were
yet to grow

Mother's Folklore

She told me it was folklore
as they cut me like a Fir tree,
and even in my falling
I still hoped to be adorned.

Amongst the chisel and the dust,
my Yule log lay down listening,
to callousness laughing
at the thought I could restore.

Their words blistered on my bark
to tell me that I couldn't,
where everything was crumbling
and my fate was dead for sure.

I smelled of sandalwood and sweetness
as they rubbed to force the sap loss,
but dirt obscured my fragrance as
they pushed me into tar.

And all my aspirations
and the things that I believed in,
were silenced when my throat was cut and
voice shed out to pour.

She told me it was folklore
to grow safe to be a Woman,
cause all they seem to tell you is
to stay down on the floor.

Flame

 Fury
was ignited,
because sweetness had no place
there
 in the dark
where rage
struck up a flame,
in me
 as I played
 with a box of matches.

When Women Tell You

I counted all my curses,
and trusted you to hear them
carrying them like timber on my way
to your sawmill.

I gathered them up for you,
as a burden hefty on my back,
straining from the wood under
its mass.

It was only when I met you there,
that you showed me how to stack them

Thinking we built honesty
not the gallows

for my neck

Listen

Listen, I don't pray to God often
            but when I do
the ghosts dragged behind me
stir up to face
my reticence,
knowing nobody heard.

The Alchemy

       Are the edges of my teeth going to cut you?
when you plunder me.
       Your
       golden girl
       Your
       little treasure
as I try to smile with my eyes
now
when you propel into the quarry of my throat,
into the crucible of me,
       while I emulate 18 Karats of pleasantries,
       and try not be anything but a gem in your alchemy.
       Because once you're on top
       of me
I'll try to burrow down
into the rock beneath my bullion back.
So my ore dissolves under the pressure of your
excavation
and the killing
that your shaft
drives
       which I now taste.

Sticky

Lonely, cross-country trips lead me to find bibles in the drawers of off
track motels
and when I'd thumb,
        flip,
        scatter through them
I'd wonder why the words wouldn't quite take,
        wouldn't quite stick
as well as the cum on the worn-out carpet.

[*Versification*, Sept 2020]

Little Man

Please complain
about the stories of your pain
so I can better understand
what motivates your hand
Little Man

Once again
Please tell me what's to gain
when you dispute the words I say
that rub you the wrong way
and ruin your day

Then you begin
to point out all the things
that make up all your wins
and undermine your sins
Little Boy

Please repeat
All the people you don't like
as your cowardice grows a stripe
when you use your hand to strike
Little Child

Please stand still
I see through the way you're billed
and will show you my own will
where power will rebuild
little man

You Burned Your Hands

I wanted to burn down your house
and all its fabrication
where you slept easy in your sin
on a bed beneath a
plastic catholic cross.
Jesus wept
hearing all your promises
as I poured gasoline on memories
and hid indifference in your walls
that painted smoothly over rot
My decision to forgive you
as you lay below your saviour
let foundations temper easy
and scorch from your guiltiness
so hot

19

Dead Bush

        You told me to hide my light under
your bushel
woven with your indignation
like a basket
        I wanted to pluck you out
of my history
like the dry heads
on the end of winters branches
        You told me you got wet
thinking it was tears
not my sweat
when I decided to cut you down
        I wanted to force you
into the dirt
that smelled just like your bullshit
to bury all your sounds

Nests

       Self doubt nests for spring
on unfertilized eggs,
where sterility and futility curve around my hopelessness.
       Wrapped up in the distrust of your dry twigs,
       It houses a
sitting bird,
waiting with a perpetual hunger,
for a future
       that will never come

Promise

               I decided to swallow the unborn
promise
like the baby
We lost
and I hoped to cast a spell on you
and let is gnaw and fester
with it
in my womb
               Where it became nothing more than a lie
that you would
drink up
speaking of devotion
when your tainted mouth touched
               mine

Seedpod

Lift it carefully.
Watch your back
Make the cinderblock balance easily when you carry it.
So when you decide drop from the bridge
you'll spin like the seedpod,
falling from the Maple tree
intact.
And when you hit the water
it will swallow you whole
to leave no trace of
your silent
splash

Punch

Please strike the space on my neck with your balled up fist.
The curve where the skin meets my shoulder
so, the place where you bite down
and breath pathetically
looks more like a bruise and not a mark where your mouth
Pretended to be a Man.

[*Versification*, **August 2020**]

Your Hair Woman

It's not the same
unless you let him pull it really hard from behind
until there's a vicious arch in
your spine.
For his visual treat.

Long locks are so feminine, and easy to grab,
and measures your glory when he's back there.

He'll hold it, twist and tug
pressing into you firmly with a
Thud, Thud, Thud.
You sultry woman!

It's not the same
on your body unless you
treat it, or tease it, or tweeze it, or bleach it
and don't complain about it please
and smile for heaven's sake.

Remember your hair,
can't be *au naturel*,
you have to keep him keen
just slide back sweetly like peaches and cream.
Because

Its not the same
darling
Unless you're just right
Just like in his wet dreams
where your pussy's shaven and tight

[*https://close to the Bone.co.uk*, **November 2020**]

25

Faith

Sometimes the leather around my neck
has the feel of comfort
I imagine prayer would.
      And those feathered words of reassurance that you blow
weakly to my ear.
Hold the murmurings of a faith
      left to die

My Forest

       I became enraged
when you tilled our land
lifted our boulders
tearing the bark from trunks
to count the rings of our worth.
       And I watched you
ravage the landscape
where you cut down and covered
those women
in a tumulus.
       My trunk grew strong
from soil that moved through my
saplings and veins
and ripened in the swell of fruit
you wished to taste
       But said nothing,
because you didn't know
I saw
you bury
my kin there
       And with my bellow
the air lifted with predictor
and stirred with a vacillation
on my foliage
as I stood resolute
for them too

Salt of the Earth

When I left my faith on the roadside
like those dated books from the attic
with your tattered
bible
My strongest realisation
was that turning my back
turned me into myself
and not
Your pillar of salt

Ceilings and Floors

Don't talk to me about your power
and your ambition
When you ask me to wipe down your
glass ceiling
and take some notes,
and smile a little
and wear some heels to raise your children
then feed your weary bones
with a supper
and a fuck
When your steps are supported on a
floor
I polished
beside your mother and your sister
who you seem to forget
while so erect in your success
where privilege started
as You were greeted when you entered the room

Apple of Their Eye

I'd met 7 men at a bar last night
and went to bed with their 7 sins
The burgundy that soiled my dress made me their 8th
assuming I was bleeding out
the burden of
Women

The Solstice

I wish they'd stop plunging women in water
or burn them like kindling and wood
or shame their blood
and the bones of their bodies.
That don't show enough in that swimsuit and don't curve enough in
that dress.

>*Why do you cry on the Solstice when the moon is full?*

he asked,

>*And weep when rocks bind your naked feet?*

Because you heaved me in your ocean
to swallow the salt from your waves.
To clean me up.
To put me right.
To drive me just so...

>*But baby,*

he interrupted

>*I just wanted to see if you'd float.*

And I'll stretch the skin of that sweet, sweet, smile,
the one you love to see,
the one you scald me to keep...

>and say

>>*I wish you'd stop plunging me in your water*
>>*or burn me like kindling and wood*
>>*you'll smell my smoke when you douse my flame*
>>*as I choke on your sea of manhood*

31

It's When

It's when you assume I'm wrong
then think to correct me
or stare blankly at my tits
then make eye contact with my cunt
and look to lick the lines of my body
when I stand up or
sit down
or speak a little too *sexy*
It's in your stare at my swollen lips
which you'll describe as pussy pink
and tight
as I hold my tongue and bite
when you place your hand on my
lower back
And despite her standing
by your side
It's when you disrespect your wife
and the privilege you describe
in the life that you '*provide*'
And then you speak of her
good luck
without you knowing that when you
touch
her smiling look under
lashes
signals
It's me she'd like to fuck

[*Cape Magazine,* 2021]

The Universe Began

   Between my legs
A universe spun with celestial moons and planets,
and at nighttime
I'd steal the luminosity from my Northern star
and touch the burn from its embers
   I'd move in dark space
were my rhythm reclaimed my flesh
as the cosmos began to shake
with a moon
that waxed and waned
   I found power in the chase
as my freedom scorched the earth
salvaging the worlds pure origin
where every man
was birthed

When You Fall Asleep

I spit in your mouth
a little
Then cover your slumber gently with a pillow where the soft cotton
shields your eyes
and the draped fabric smothers your face
So I can
rush to touch vigorously the salacity of my skin.
That your skin
on mine
can't satisfy

Fuss

A tempest kicks up a fuss in me
as hands lap against the shores of my flesh
where the weathers turn sounds a warning,
like a siren on the rocks.

And I stand and feel the eye form,
storming a fiery burn in my gut
Disregarding being called a *Lady*
and welcoming your label *Slut*

My tempest kicks up a fuss in me
Despite all the violation and smite
where I reach to feel the waves thrust
as the rain it comes in sight.

One thing is certain
within my body and my thighs
my power pulls my craving
with a summoning roll of my eyes.

The tempest rolls in to greet me
A woman's hedonism I will get
As I embrace the rhythm of the ocean
Where I'm sure to get soaking wet

Scuffed Knees

        When I kneel down to pray
I think of taking you in
my mouth
        Drinking from your aspergillum
blessed by God
himself

Hurricane

        Stiff against the torrent of rain that casts veins of lightning
in a sky of pure cinereal shades
        I summon the electricity
from the hills where they scratch
towards my silhouette
standing stark and looming
        Their touch set me alight
as sparks flew between flesh and bone
towards my heart of wood
and launched fire from the fuel
of my
        carnality.

Rage

They say rage is like a fire
and its burn leaves a mark on you
where ash and soot
conceal
a catastrophe
set to blaze

Ritual Burning

And it erupts
to catch easily in flames,
as the wind picks up the loose grasses with sparks
which chatter and crack from
all of my hesitations.

They disappear against the black of night,
irradiated ahead of me on the footpath
where all things forward
and all the things backwards
Sprint in flares that lick in a line.

And my tenacity exudes upwards
As ashes fly away and coals consume my bare feet.

They do not scorch,
but simmer from a baptism of fire
where fury
and resilience
radiate

Epilogue

Baptism by Fire, is a poetry story inspired by the symbolism[i] and hetropatriarchal norms found in the stories of Greek and Roman mythology. The work focuses on key ideas around the representation of women that form part of these tales in a modern present day context. The work looks at a collection of stories told through the life cycle of a woman through her journey to self-discovery. The work does not reference mythology directly, but juxtaposes symbols and key beliefs in relation to present day societal norms. This begs the question as to the progression of present society and the perception of women, and touches on the modern entrenched belief that salvation can only be found in absolving power to God[ii].

In mythology there is often a double standard[iii]; women are portrayed as deceitful and manipulative[iv], their actions are often described as the cause of men's downfall[v]. Men appear to be powerless to their seduction and women are depicted as sinister in their motives[vi] to lead men astray. Women are deemed to be the objects of men's lust[vii], forcing men to use their physical vigour to overpower them through the act of domestication and strength. Men are depicted as heroic, and the control of women is therefore seen to be an act of bravery[viii]. Oppression forms part of male liberation, it functions as part of a power dynamic where the act of conquering further empowers them. By overpowering her, he fortifies his strength to overpower his enemies too. She is the function of internal discord, and the oppression allows him to ensure her power does not cause his downfall.

Baptism by Fire draws on mythology by highlighting women as objects of male desire. A woman's own desire is deemed to be an anomaly[ix], and should she act on it, she would undermine the male hierarchy by going against the natural order[x]. She is seen to tarnish not only herself, but him and the community. Men use misogynistic acts to shame woman[xi]. They believe that as the male heroes, they are required to pacify woman to restore order. Her desire is seen to be dangerous in leading the male hero to lose control. Men therefore use force to subdue her through acts of violence[xii].

Often women in mythology are punished, banished and killed because of their sexual appetite, their love, or even their own rape[xiii]. Women are required to service men, and should she reject him, she would be subject to blame, shame and chastisement. Consent does not form part of the desire exchange[xiv]. In Baptism by Fire, a correlation is made between the stories of mythology and the stories where punishment changes a women's form[xv]. The book focuses specifically on the idea of trees[xvi], where the symbolism is juxtaposed with the weight and burden of wood.

Baptism by Fire is a book about overcoming destruction and pursuing sexual awakening and in turn, power. Should a man acknowledge a woman's appetite for pleasure, he would be opening himself to the recognition of her own power and the ownership of her body. He would be forced to acknowledge that she is powerful to overcome his strength. Should she reclaim her female sexual appetite, she would contradict his idea of domestication.

Baptism by Fire looks at the story of men attempting to undermine and manipulate a female protagonists body in their pursuit of their own power[xvii]. By deeming her to be the property of the hero, she is within reach of the male grasp. Her power lies in reclaiming her flesh, her pleasure and desire, which men feel they need to control. By releasing the belief that God will save her, she is able to recognise the power within herself as her own saviour, and dissemble the need for a hero to rescue her. It is therefore through the act of salvaging her body, that she recognises her true power, which has the potential to overthrow her male captors. This rebirth would ultimately lead to a male downfall as her amorous desire and the release of shame is seen to be the biggest threat to male strength.

41

Annotation:

---

[i] Tapestry and knotting; A typically feminine task, tapestry weaving is one of the few creative outlets for Greek women. Mythology depicts key female characters performing the act of weaving; Helen is introduced in the *Iliad* weaving a tapestry depicting the battle she inspired. Clytemnestra manipulates her husband as she threads a luxurious tapestry beneath his feet. Circe the witch, is introduced in the *Odyssey* weaving and singing amongst tamed beasts. Penelope repeatedly weaves and unpicks a shroud to purposefully delay her remarriage, and a tongueless Philomela reveals her rape by her brother in law Tereus, by weaving to communicate his crime.

Boxes and wood: The first woman Pandora was created as punishment to man after Prometheus stole fire from the Gods. Although beautiful, her representation is indicative of deception, trickery and chaos, having released troubles to mankind and leaving only hope.

Gallows, Swinging and Hanging: Hanging was considered a specifically female act of suicide and punishment. A number of key female characters and myths depict the act of hanging; Jocasta, mother of Oedipus, kills herself by hanging in an act of remorse. Odysseus hangs slave women as punishment for taking lovers amongst suitors in his absence. Danaos' daughters threaten to hang themselves with their virginal belts, unless they are granted refuge in Argos. Archilochus' poetry depicts the daughters of Lycambes driven to hanging. In conjunction with the act of hanging, the depictions of the myths of Phaedra depict swinging in conjunction with her inevitable suicide. The juxtaposition between swinging and hanging has been likened to that of the act of her death and Aiora rituals were Athenian young women would sit on the swing to commemorate Erigone's unfortunate destiny, and at times forming a symbol of physiological and psychological hysteria.

Fruit and flowers; Ovid's depiction illustrates Phaedra describing herself in love as a 'young colt being broken, ripe fruit being plucked as a first rose'. In light of this symbolism, the Romans saw roses as a symbol of death, rebirth, and growth associated with youth. Lyric poems associate erotic bodies with flowers. Poets such as Ibycus and Anacreon cast bodies adorned with flowers, and as such flowers represent sexuality and eroticism.

[ii] As woman are seen to be the instigators of original sin, likened to mythology's Pandora, salvation to some degree exists only to absolve power to the masculine. The recent development of Feminist philosophy in regard to religion questions traditions, practices and texts through a critique on gender roles and representations in a traditionally patriarchal context. The idea that absolution and freedom can only be attained through repentance is complex. The identity and representation of woman is thus brought to question, especially in light of liberation through sensuality of sexual freedom beyond procreation.

[iii] The Gods' pursuit of female mortals is not deemed to hold the same shame as Goddesses consorting with mortal men. If Goddesses were able to pursue mortal men in the same way as Gods, this would indicate equality between both and recognize a level playing field in terms of their amorous desires. Such recognition would result in the male giving up their power in light of equality.

[iv] Clytemnestra takes a lover when her husband King Agamemnon is away in Troy. Upon his return, she murders him in an act of violent eroticism and appears to rejoice in quasi-sexual delight. Prior to his death, she manipulated him to commit an act of *hybris* as she threaded her tapestry at his feet. Her manipulative character is further reinforced in her speech in Aeschylus' play, *Agamemnon*, revealing the murder as an act of vengeance for her daughter Iphigenia, whom Agamemnon sacrificed to obtain favourable winds for his expedition to Troy.

ᵛ Helen is seen to be the cause of the Trojan War as she chose a young virile lover over her husband, family and kingdom

ᵛⁱ Pandora, is described as a πῆμα (*pêma*), a 'bane' upon men despite having been created to be beautiful, with a 'lovely form', 'golden necklaces' and a head 'crowned with flowers.' It noted that within her there were placed 'lies and crafty words and a deceitful nature' contrived 'by the will of loud-thundering Zeus'.

ᵛⁱⁱ The Rape of Spartan Queen Leda, is forced at the hands of Zeus who transformed into a swan. It is often depicted in fresco as a romantic conquest. This is in stark contrast to the literary interpretation of Yeats, retelling from the perspective of Leda as a traumatic, forceful and violent event (*Leda and the Swan*). This example is typical of mythology in that it frames, often traumatic, assault as amorous vanquishing, which for the victim, should be deemed honourable as it would have occurred from a god himself.

ᵛⁱⁱⁱ Consideration to the depiction of woman as monsters or beasts can be likened to the view that females are inherently agents of chaos. Misogyny is a belief system that women are inferior, subservient, and unequal. The use of symbols to depict woman as monsters further normalises the belief that woman are inhuman, unequal and often the scapegoat. This dehumanises the validity of female identity. Beastly and inhuman characters are reflected in, Scylla, Charybdis, the Harpies, Medusa, Empusa, the Furies, Graeae, Lamia, the witch Circe and her niece Medea.

ⁱˣ When the gods free Odysseus after being held captive by the Goddess Calypso on her island, she remarks that 'the gods are cruel and jealous, for they never let goddesses take mortal lovers for long' (*Odyssey* V. 116-44).

ˣ Clytemnestra expresses her sexual nature freely and is therefore seen to pose a threat to society and her husband. The sexual nature of woman is inherently seen to be a primary threat to destroy men's status. She is seen to be a non-ideal woman considered destructive by the male oriented society.

[xi] The poet Archilochus narrated his seduction of two unmarried sisters which was intended to shame both them and their father who had slighted Archilochus. This resulted in all three hanging by suicide.

[xii] In *Odyssey* X, Circe's drugs have failed to bewitch Odysseus, he then threatens her with a sword and overpowers her physically. They go to bed together, where the physical domination becomes sexual. Violent sexual domination by men is normalized in both Greek and Roman comedy plays referencing rapes, torn hair, ripped clothes, and the woman's distress. Various stories depict woman having been raped, overtaken or killed as a result of having rejected male characters forceful advances.

[xiii] Ovid's version of Medusa depicts her as beautiful. Despite her oath of chastity to serve Athena, her beauty drew the attention of the sea god Poseidon. The story depicts a brutal attack and rape by Poseidon inside of Athena's temple, where instead of being deemed the victim, she is blamed and punished. Cursed for Poseidon's deeds, she is transformed into a hideous monster whose appearance turns onlookers to stone. After many years, the Greek hero Perseus is sent to look for Medusa and kill her where he uses her head as a trophy and weapon to turn others to stone.

[xiv] Greek law did not distinguish between consensual and non-consensual extra-marital sex, or rape, with married or unmarried woman. The law was only concerned with the marital status of the woman as a means to identify who the woman's legal owner was. This would indicate who was due reparations for the crime against his property.

Metamorphosis and the ability to change form is a key element in Greek mythology. This ability is a major theme in the stories of Arachne, Zeus, and Daphne.

xvi In Greek and Roman myth the metamorphosis of women is often portrayed as a form of escape or in some instances punishment. A focus has been placed on those stories which reflect the transformation associated with trees.

The myth of Apollo and Daphne is seen as a depiction of a predator in pursuit of lust. She is saved in the act of transformation into a laurel tree. The myth is portrayed as a battle between chastity and sexual desire. The transformation appears to be her only form of escape, and to sacrifice her body, is in fact the only way to save herself when the god grant her prayers (Ovid. *Met.*1.525*ff.*).

Pitys pursuit of Pans advances is saved when she is transformed into a pine. He tried to seduce Syrinx who tries to escape by requesting help from river nymphs. She was transformed into reeds, which Pan cut into lengths and turned into flutes. When he played the instrument, the notes frightened *maenads*, female followers of Dionysus, into the woodland.

Marked by his oversized permanent erection, Priapus' failed attempt to rape the goddess Hestia, lead to the pursuit of Lotis. Pity from the Gods tranformed Lotis into a lotus plant.

After Phaethon's death, his mother Clymene searched the earth for his limbs and bones. She and her daughters, the Heliades, wept for their brother so much that their tears hardened into amber. Their grief turned them into poplar trees near the river Eridanus.

After a concerned Philyra bore Chiron the Centaur, she asked Zeus to change her form. Granting her wish he transformed her into a linden tree.

The story of Baucis and Philemon, much like biblical Lot and his wife, were granted a wish from Zeus to be guardians of a temple and die together. Upon their death they were transformed into intertwining oak and linden trees.

Hamadryad's woodland nymphs are a particular type of *dryad* who live in trees bonded to them at birth. It's believed they are the actual tree and not simply the entities or spirits. At their birth, pines or oaks spring from the ground and tower over the land, and at their death, the tree withers too, and 'the life of the Nymph and of the tree leave the light of the sun together.' (*Homeric Hymn to Aphrodite* 256-72).

[xvii] The Rape of Persephone is a mythological tale of the abduction of the springtime goddess by Hades, king of the Underworld. A story of stolen innocence occurs as a result of having been sanctioned by Zeus himself. Her mother Demeter, was not informed of the plan where Zeus decided the fate of his daughter to advance the interests of both households. A daughter is the property of her father until she is ready to be handed over to a new household. This myth resulted in the story surrounding the creation of the seasons, as Demeter mourns over Persephone's time in the Underworld. The pain is centred around how inseparable the connection of love between mother and daughter is, even in the face of a gross injustice where her body is used to advance the interests of two households.

Printed in Great Britain
by Amazon

57515402R00037